PUFFIN BO

The Pirate's Secret Joke Book

Hee-hee-heave
And ho-ho-hove
Me ha-ha-hearties

Shiver your timbers with this
treasure trove of pirate fun,
brought to you from across
the seven seas to get you
jigging in the rigging.
Pira-tickle your
funny bones today!

Some other books by Shoo Rayner

THE CHRISTMAS STOCKING JOKE BOOK
THE LITTLE BOOK OF NEW YEAR'S
RESOLUTIONS

Fiction

SANTA'S DIARY

For younger readers
Picture Books

CAT IN A FLAP
HEY DIDDLE DIDDLE
NOAH'S ABC

Ready, Steady, Read

CYRIL'S CAT: CHARLIE'S NIGHT OUT
CYRIL'S CAT AND THE BIG SURPRISE
CYRIL'S CATS: MOUSE PRACTICE

The Pirate's Secret Joke Book

Yo-ho-ho and a Lottle of Fun

Shoo Rayner

PUFFIN BOOKS

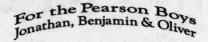

For the Pearson Boys
Jonathan, Benjamin & Oliver

PUFFIN BOOKS

Published by the Penguin Group
Penguin Books Ltd, 27 Wrights Lane, London W8 5TZ, England
Penguin Putnam Inc., 375 Hudson Street, New York, New York 10014, USA
Penguin Books Australia Ltd, Ringwood, Victoria, Australia
Penguin Books Canada Ltd, 10 Alcorn Avenue, Toronto, Ontario, Canada M4V 3B2
Penguin Books (NZ) Ltd, Private Bag 102902, NSMC, Auckland, New Zealand

Penguin Books Ltd, Registered Offices: Harmondsworth, Middlesex, England

First published 1999
3

Copyright © Shoo Rayner, 1999
All rights reserved

The moral right of the author/illustrator has been asserted

Laserset by the Author

Made and printed in England by Clays Ltd, St Ives plc

British Library Cataloguing in Publication Data
A CIP catalogue record for this book is available from the British Library

ISBN 0–140–37518–X

Contents

We're coming to get you!

Beware the Pirate Sign

You never know when the call will come. Sitting at your breakfast table, opening the post, what looks like a birthday card from your Aunty Agnes is a fake. While you look for the five-pound note that you hope she put in for you, a disc of black card drops out and lands in your cereal bowl ...

You have been called to join the Secret Pirate Society. The disc is their sign and there is no escape from it. They will come to fetch you when you least expect it: in the middle of the night when you are all tucked up and dreaming of Christmas, on the way to Granny's for a summer holiday, even while you are changing your library books. Watch out! Lurking behind the encyclopedias, hairy pirate crews are waiting to pounce and drag you off to a life of crime, swashbuckling and (it has to be said) romance! It will be a hard life and you will need a sense of humour, so what better than a few piratical jokes and quizzes to pass the time until they come for you?

In the Navy

The Royal Navy is the pirates' only real enemy, which is surprising because generally they are a pretty useless lot! You can understand why when you look at a cross-section of a fighting ship and its crew.

Navy officers are usually the skinny younger sons of the rich and famous. They would much rather be at home with their mummies and their teddy bears!

Petty officers are the tough elder sons of village squires. Since it is they who really run the ship, they would rather be the captain.

The ratings are the poor fools who were found blind drunk in pubs or just hit on the head by press-gangs,* to wake up on board ship, miles from home, enlisted in the Royal Navy.

* Press-gangs roamed the pubs and the streets looking for men who they could 'press' into the Navy. If they gave you some money then it was said that you had 'taken the King's Shilling'. You would be marched off to a ship and not let out until the ship was at sea. There was no time to say goodbye to Mummy!

The Joys of Piracy

What's the best thing about being a pirate? You can do just what you want to do and no one is going to tell you off for doing it. If you are caught, you might get hanged from the yard-arm, but in the mean time you can do what you want, eat what you want and wear what you want!

What do big, strong pirates eat?

Mussels!

What do you call a handsome, happy, good-tempered pirate?

A complete failure!

Which pirate wore the biggest boots?

The one with the biggest feet!

Why did the pirate wear pink, spotty braces?
To hold his trousers up!

Parrot to be friends with (no one else will be friends!)

Hat for Keeping secrets under

determined Look

Jolly Roger World Tour

Swiss Army cutlass (very useful when splicing the main-brace!)

Hook for fishing

Boots to quake in

Knobbly Knees to Knock

swimming trunks

Why did the pirate wear red trousers?
Because he'd spilt tomato ketchup on them.

Leg Monthly

Incorporating
THE HOOK GAZETTE

HARRY HOOKS A HEFTY HADDOCK

Harold Whinge, known to his friends as *Horrid Harry*, sent in this picture of the humungus haddock that he caught while trailing his hooked left arm out of the porthole in his cabin.

'I was trying a new kind of bait,' said Harry. 'Since I've entered for the world hooking championships, I won't say what the bait was. It's my secret weapon!'

WHAT THE DOCTOR SAID

You keep on sending in your medical stories. Here are a couple about tactful surgeons.

Well, the bad news is that I cut off your good leg by mistake; the good news is that the other one is getting better!

Well, the bad news is that I had to cut both your legs off; the good news is that the captain wants to buy your slippers!

Letters to the Editor

Dear Sir,

Last month you printed a story about me and how I lost my hand in a fight with a clockwork alligator. That story is so old that Long John Silver still had two legs when it was first told. The truth is that I lost it in a duel with a fearsome fairy called Tinker Bell. I suppose it just doesn't make such a good story.

Yours etc., Hook (Captain)   *Ooops, sorry! Ed.*

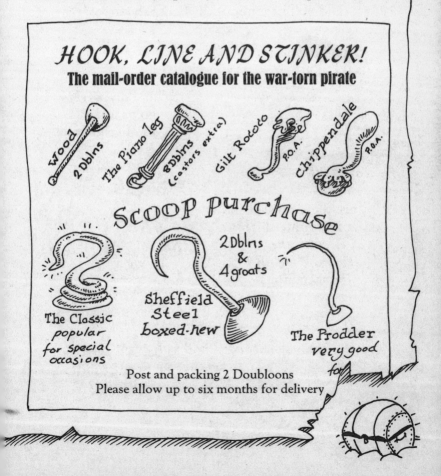

HOOK, LINE AND STINKER!

The mail-order catalogue for the war-torn pirate

Wood 2 Dblns

The Piano leg 3 Dblns (castors extra)

Gilt Rococo P.O.A.

Chippendale P.O.A.

Scoop purchase

The Classic popular for special occasions

Sheffield Steel boxed-new 2 Dblns & 4 groats

The Prodder very good for

Post and packing 2 Doubloons
Please allow up to six months for delivery

Pollyfillers

Did you hear about the Scottish parrot?
His name is
Jock McCaw.

Where do parrots
go to learn?
At a Polly Technic!

Why are there no aspirins
on board pirate ships?
*Because the
parrots ate 'em all.)
(Paracetamol.)*

What is a parrot's
favourite food?
Pollyfiller!

The Game of Pirates

Have you ever played the game of pirates? It's a lot of fun.
All you need are the things to make islands.

One of the best places to play it is in
the gym at school, especially if you
can get the ropes out.

You need to build a course,
made up of islands, which
could be mats,
cushions,
springboards, boxes –
you name it,
anything that you
can jump into and
out of or on to and
off again.

Basically the course
is laid out in a
circular fashion so
that you can jump
around, from one
island to another,
without touching
the floor. This is
very important, as
the floor is the deep
blue sea and if you
put your foot in it you
are instantly drowned!

The person who is chosen to
be the pirate then counts to
twenty, so that everyone else can
choose their starting positions. The
pirate can now decide which island to land
on and the action can begin!

If the pirate touches any of his victims they join the pirate crew and help to catch the rest.

The winner is the last person to be caught by the pirates. That person has to be caught to win, though! No getting out of that one! The winner is now the new pirate and counts to twenty while everyone else gets back on the islands.

If at any time you should put your foot in the water and are drowned, you will have to sit out the rest of the game.

You could play this outside and mark areas to be islands in the dust or the snow or whatever. If there is a tree around from which you can swing on a rope, that will make it much more piratey!

You could base a course around a climbing frame in the garden. The more you use your imagination, the more fun it is. Don't be too rough, though, and don't make islands from precious or dangerous things!

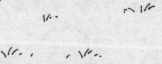

All the Animals

It wasn't just pirates on board pirate ships. With a hold full of supplies, a ship attracts rats and mice, and where there are rats and mice, then a cat is needed.

Other strange pets made their way on board too: monkeys were always a favourite, and there was also the passing bird life.

Sometimes there were children on board.

They were *buoys and gulls!*

Why was the cat thrown into the water?

It was on fire!

Don't even think about it!

Knock, knock.
Who's there?
Cattle.
Cattle who?
Cat'll purr if you stroke it!

MMMMM...
a double
doubloon.

Why did the pirate feed his cat on pieces of eight?

Because he liked to keep something in the kitty!

My cat can speak in a foreign language.

Go on then, make it say something.

Woof!

What do you do to a drowning mouse?

Give it mouse to mouse resuscitation!

What do you get if you cross a rat with a woodpecker?

A Rat-a-tat-tat!

What's brown, has four legs and a hairy chest?

A PiRat!

now that is a hairy chest!

The very first crow's nest was so called because a large black bird made its nest in it. The poor creature went completely mad through the loneliness of the long voyage. It turned into a *Raven Lunatic!*

What is a crowbar?
A place where birds go to drink.

What do you call a pirate with a seagull on his head? *Cliff!*

Did you hear about the cockerel who lived on board a pirate ship? They called him Robinson, *because he crew so!*

What do you mean piracy is illegal? There're no sick birds on this ship!

Crock-a-diddle-doo!

Pirate Wordsearch

Look carefully at the letters in the boxes below and see if you can find the hidden words.
The answers are on page 94.

H	E	T	A	R	I	P	R	Y
D	L	O	G	F	D	S	O	L
Z	L	U	V	B	N	N	G	L
X	L	R	J	S	G	V	E	O
L	U	F	G	B	L	K	R	J
X	C	B	O	N	E	S	W	R
D	G	N	O	L	O	A	J	K
M	N	H	O	J	V	Z	R	O
S	I	L	V	E	R	B	W	D

These are the words you are looking for.

BEARD – LONG JOHN SILVER –
JOLLY ROGER – WAVE – PIRATE –
GOLD – GULL – BONES.

The Art of Piracy

The real art of piracy lies in cowardice, greed and deception! Now you, the reader of this book, are, of course, a dear, sweet person and have never had a bad thought enter your brain in all your life. *(Hem, hem!)*

If, on the other hand, you want to be an arty pirate, then here are some ideas for you.

First you need to design your own pirate emblem. It could be the skull and crossbones or something a bit more gruesome. You can then use your emblem on hats, flags and badges.

where can you find a Coward?

Try "Yellow" Pages!

You can make a hat from two sheets of card. Cut out the shape and staple round the edges. *(Staples are much stronger than glue on a job like this, but do mind your fingers!)*

Now you can paint or draw your design on the front and decorate by gluing on feathers, milk-bottle tops, buttons, stickers, etc.

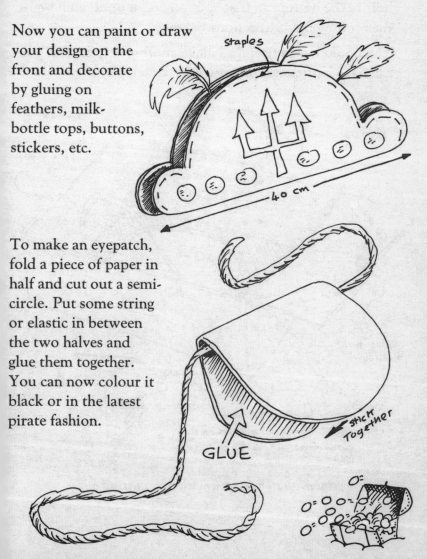

staples

40 cm

To make an eyepatch, fold a piece of paper in half and cut out a semi-circle. Put some string or elastic in between the two halves and glue them together. You can now colour it black or in the latest pirate fashion.

GLUE

stick Together

Why not make your own pirate ship? Here are some ideas for a ship that you can put on and sail around in. You could even wear it to a fancy-dress party.

You will need a box that is large enough to 'wear'. Cut a hole in the bottom so that you can pull it up to your waist, then follow the instructions below.

You could help a friend to make another ship so that you can have battles and practise your attack plans.

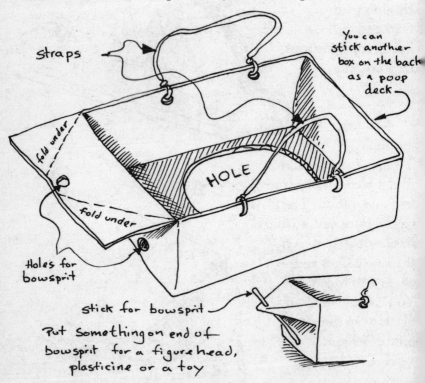

straps

You can stick another box on the back as a poop deck

fold under

fold under

HOLE

Holes for bowsprit

stick for bowsprit

Put something on end of bowsprit for a figurehead, plasticine or a toy

(Ask a grown-up to help you with any cutting out.)

Toilet rolls

Jolly Roger

NAVY HAT

NAVY SHIP

Black and yellow stripes

Seasickness

It's a sad fact but true: all that heaving around in stormy seas can make you feel quite queasy. The quality of the food will no doubt add to your problems, and as for hygiene, well, there are all sorts of horrible diseases lurking in the bilges!

What's the best cure
for seasickness?
Bolt your food down!

HMMMM...
Very interesting!

What's seasickness?
*It's what a doctor does
all day long!*

You remind me of the sea.

Why, because of my wild
and stormy nature?

No, because you make me sick!

What are you giving the captain for Christmas?

I don't know. I gave him scurvy last year.

What happened to the happy pirate?
He had a hearty-tack!

Ha-ha haaarg!

What do you call a pirate who's been left floating in a barrel?
Bob!

Did you hear about the seasick pirate who jumped overboard?
His medicine had to be taken in water!

Armed to the Teeth

When your job involves robbing and stealing from treasure ships, then weapons are the tools of your trade. As you swing alongside a merchant ship whose holds are stuffed with gold and diamonds, you will want to fire off a few shots from your cannon, just to scare the crew a bit. Then, when you get on board, you will have to put your trust in your cutlass and dagger. (*Actually, if you look fierce enough, the crew on board the merchant ship will be so scared that you won't have to do any fighting at all!*)

Did you know that there was once a pirate whose reputation was so fierce that he was blamed for killing the Dead Sea!

What does a cannonball do when it's not being fired?
It looks round!

What does a ship's cannon shoot?
Sea shells!

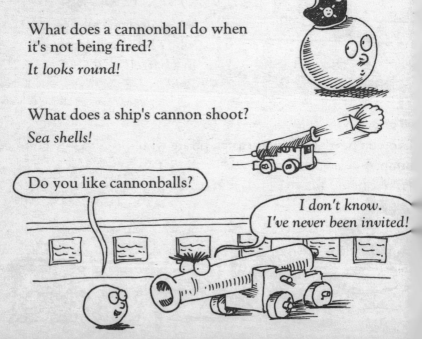

Do you like cannonballs?

I don't know. I've never been invited!

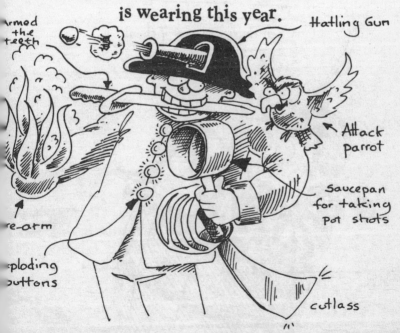

How was gunpowder invented?
In a flash!

Up the Crow's Nest

I'm homesick.
But this is your home now.
I know. I'm sick of it.
Why did the pirate cover himself in grease at night?
Because he wanted to get up oily in the morning!

Swashbuckling

Swashbuckling is something that you cannot learn. You have to be born to it. You have to be carefree, wickedly handsome and prepared to spit in the face of adversity!

You don't need a swash and you don't need a buckle, but you do need to be able to put the two together in wild and interesting ways!

A pirate who buckled his Swash,
Thought that his opponents were tosh,
Till a big Navy cruiser,
Took a shot at the bruiser,
And sunk him right there and then ... splosh!

There's an unwritten law about life on board a ship, and that is that arguments get settled on land, when the ship reaches a port. That's why alongside every harbour there is a *Duel Carriageway!*

What does a swashbuckling teacher say?

Don't just stand there, slay something!

Take Your Punishment!

If you are a lily-livered softy, then now is the time to jump ship. Have you ever thought about the sort of people who are attracted to the pirate life? Well, they tend to be a bit rough: thieves, robbers, blackmailers, deserters and just plain murderers.

Keeping such a crew in order requires strict discipline and that demands severe punishment for anyone breaking the pirate code of 'Be kind to your neighbour'.

There were some pretty terrible punishments to endure, not just the bad food! There were the floggings with the cat-o'-nine-tails* or keelhauling,* you might be set adrift or left to rot on a desert island, or hanged from the yard-arm.*

What do you say when you are
lashed with the cat-o'-nine-tails?

Mee-ow-ow-ow-ow-ow-ow-ow-ow-ow!

---

*The cat-o'-nine-tails was a whip with nine lashes on it, and keelhauling involved dragging a man on a rope under the hull and keel of the ship, which was usually covere͏ in sharp barnacles. A yard-arm is a piece of wood that crosses the mast, from which th͏ sails are hung.

Knock, knock.
Who's there?
Dishwasher.
Dishwasher who?
Dishwasher way
I shpoke after the
captain hit me!

We've been marooned.

I'm feeling blue.

I'm in the pink.

Well, I'm in the red!

Bye-bye!

What do you get hanging
from the yard-arm?

Sore arms!

Treasure Island

Here is a good game to play with a friend when you are on the midnight watch and your ship is stuck in the Doldrums.

You will need a sheet of paper each. Without letting your opponent see, you each draw two grids of thirty-six squares, six squares along the top marked 1–6, and six down the side marked A–F.

Now you each design an island inside one of your grids. On the island mark an 'H' for harbour and 'T' for treasure; also draw two skulls and crossbones. You can put these features wherever you like. Of course, you can do lots more drawing if you like.

Toss a coin to see who starts (doubloons are best!).

Take it in turns to call out the grid references of squares (e.g. the top left-hand square will be A1). Your opponent must tell you what is drawn in that square on their map. Mark down what they tell you on the grid that you have drawn.

You must find the harbour first before looking for the treasure. If you call out a square that has the sea or the coast in it, your opponent must tell you if the harbour is north, south, east or west of that point.

If you call out the treasure square before landing in the harbour then your opponent mustn't tell you that the treasure is there and must say 'land' instead.

When you have found the harbour, you can look for the treasure. If you don't call out the treasure square, your opponent must tell you whether the treasure is north, south, east or west of the square you have chosen.

*The Doldrums is a place near the Equator where the trade winds cancel each other out so that it is very calm. Not good for sailing!

With skill you can then work out where the treasure square is. The first one to find the treasure is, of course, the winner.

And what about the skulls and crossbones? Well, if you call out one of these squares, then you miss a turn. Alternatively you could be made to perform a forfeit like walking the plank … *Have fun!*

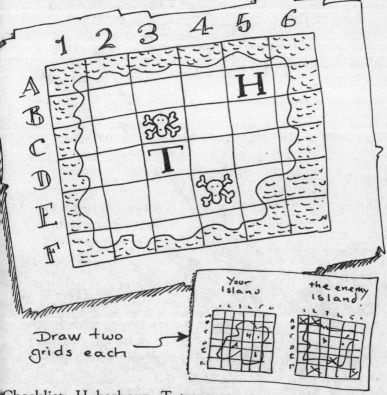

Draw two grids each →

Your Island   *the enemy Island!*

Checklist: H–harbour T–treasure

Two skulls and crossbones

(You can make the grid much bigger and put more details in if you like.)

The Seven Seas

What did the
pirate say when
the sea dried up?

*I haven't an ocean.
(A notion.)*

What did the sea say to
the sand?

Nothing, it just waved!

If an ocean is 1,000 miles wide, how far can you sail into it?

You can only sail 500 miles into it; after that you are sailing out of it!

Is it dangerous to swim on a full stomach?

It's safer to swim in water.

How many fathoms are there in a metre?

I don't know. Fathom it out yourself!

What do you do if you get stuck on board a ship?

Call a taxi crab.

Treasure Trove

Did you hear about the pirates who raided a ship and even stole the bath?

They wanted to make a clean getaway!

Did you know that pirates believed in give and take?

Give people a hard time and take everything they've got!

What is a pirate's favourite instrument?

The lute!

Did you hear about the pirates who raided a ship and stole everything except the soap and towels?

They were dirty so-and-sos!

Figureheads

How do you carve a figurehead?
Whittle by whittle!

Why do ships have carpenters?
So that every day will be plane sailing!

Trident-tested →

Sea
Lion

King of
the Sea

Yo!

King of
the Surf

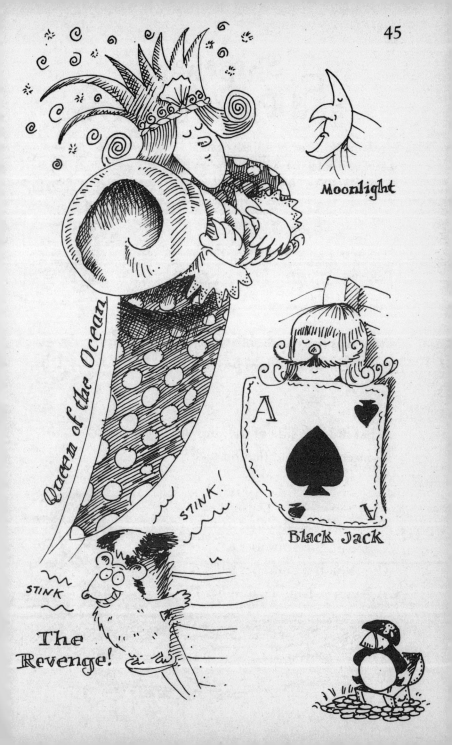

Moonlight

Queen of the Ocean

Black Jack

STINK!

STINK

The Revenge!

45

Shipshape and Pirate Fashion

Pirate ships are really quite economical.
They do 300 miles to the galleon!

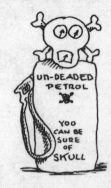

When is a ship like a fall of snow?
When it's adrift.

Why was the pirate ship always high and dry?
Because it was made of beech wood. (Beach.)

What did one side of the ship say to the other?
I'll meet you round the front.

'Come in, boat number 61!'
'Come in, boat number 61!'
'Come in, boat number 61!'
'Are you in trouble, number 19?'

What do all ships weigh,
regardless of their size?

Their anchors.

What sits at the bottom
of the sea and shakes?

A nervous wreck.

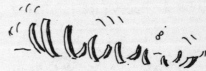

How do you stop water
from getting into a ship?

Don't pay the water bill!

When is a ship in love?

When it's attached to a buoy.

A prehistoric pirate ship was
found lying on the bottom
of the Spanish main.

It was a Tyrannosaurus wreck.

How does a ship show affection?

It hugs the shore.

Up the Crow's Nest Again

What would you do if you saw ten great big, hairy pirates coming towards you?

I'd hope that they were going to a fancy-dress party!

There was a big, strong pirate called Pete who walked into a bar and started to cry.

It was an iron bar!

Well, that's one in the eye!

Why didn't the
pirate get hurt
when a barrel
landed on his head?

*It was a barrel of
light ale!*

Why do
pirates get
angry?

It's all the rage!

Did you hear that the
captain's wife ran
away? He took her for
a mate and she's turned
into a skipper!

Did someone
say Kipper?

Skull & Crossword

Here's a little puzzle to rack your brains.
Answers on page 94.

Across

1   Pirate. Two dollar earrings, one dollar each ear!
6   This will probably end up round your neck!
7   Maybe laid in crow's nest.
8   Mayday.
9   The bosun sits in one of these.
10   What your neck becomes in 6 across.
14   The person who would paint your pirate portrait.

Down

1   These might be buried by a sea dog.
2   What you do with a pair of 1 downs.
3   Favourite pirate pet. From Barbary coast?
4   'I see no ships.' Well, take this off then.
5   He's very jolly.
9   What the captain might wear with tails on.
10   It's all around the ship.
11   Vermin. 12 down should catch it!
12   The purr-fect pirate pet.
13   You probably want a large gold hoop in this.

51

The Long Arm of the Law

All this gallivanting round the high seas, partying every night, robbing and stealing and generally being not very nice, is going to catch up with you.

You may think you can get away with it, but you can never trust your shipmates. If there's a reward on offer, someone will turn you in. So much for honour among thieves!

In the courtroom you will have to face both the judge and your wicked past. Woe betide you should the judge put on his black cap to pass your sentence. You're on your way to the executioner!

But at least you will have had your day in court.

Why did the pirate grow a beard?

So that no one could call him a bare-faced liar.

What did the pirates say when they heard that their judge was only four foot tall?

He's a small thing sent to try us.

They'll wish they'd never said that!

What do you call a judge with no fingers?
Justice Thumbs.

What does a judge say after work?
This has been a trying day.

Hangman's Corner

What do you call a pirate
with a price on his head?

Wanted.

What did the condemned pirate say when the firing squad shot him through the chest?

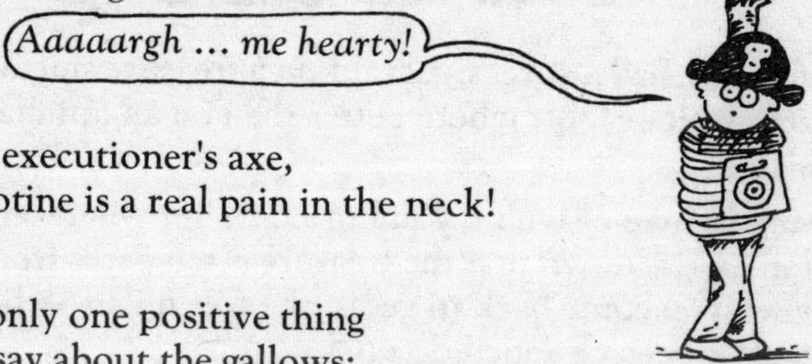

Aaaaargh ... me hearty!

Like the executioner's axe,
the guillotine is a real pain in the neck!

There's only one positive thing
you can say about the gallows:

NOOSE IS GOOD NOOSE!

What does the hangman
like to read?

The noose papers!

Treasure Maps

If you've had a successful raid on a treasure ship and need to hide your loot, where better than on an uninhabited island?

Make a map of where you buried it, but whatever you do don't write down that the treasure is ten paces from a tree; when you come back to get it, the tree might well have died or been chopped down!

Draw your map on something strong; tissue paper is not going to last very long in a pirate's coat pocket!

This is the captain speaking.
The good news is that there
is sunny weather, a strong breeze
and all's well with the ship.
The bad news is that we're lost!

First find the pig rock, then go forty paces N.E. to the palm trees, then go due west sixty paces to where the mermaid combs her hair. Now go S.W. twenty paces. This will bring you back to pig rock... Dig here!

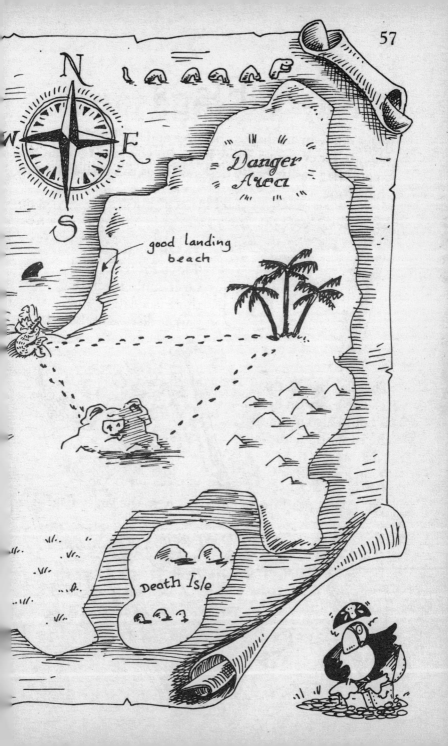

Danger Area

good landing
beach

Death Isle

Flags

Flags come in all shapes and sizes and are for flying up high, to let everyone know just who you are. You can read a good flag easily; badly designed flags can easily be read the wrong way.

This flag says:
'I love Pretty Polly.'
Or it could mean that
there is a dangerous
parrot disease on board.

This flag means that
it's wash day on board.
It could also mean that
the captain's name is
Nicholas.
(Knicker-less!)

What did the happy flag say to the angry flag?

Don't get in
such a flap!

Grrr!

This is the Red Duster. It is the flag of a British merchant ship. To a pirate it says, 'This ship needs a good dusting up!'

UNDER NEW MANAGEMENT!

This is the flag on the same ship after the pirates have given it a good dusting!

Dentist needed on board →

You're flagging, boy!

I know! I've been *waving these things* all day.

Signals and Messages

The simplest signals can be hung from the yard-arm.

For instance, if the food is bad
this is a clear signal to the cook! ——→

Messages can be carried
in many ways. They can be
tied to an arrow and shot.

GOT YOU!

They can be tied to a pigeon's leg.

I LOVE YOU PRETTY POLLY.

They can be put into a bottle.
*(Make sure it's watertight and
provides helpful information
for the finder.)*

Help Me!

Messages can get a bit damp.

If you are worried about anyone else reading your messages then you can always write them in code.

TO CAP – TIN   BLACK BEARD.

MEET   YOU   IN   SANTA   CRUISE.

British Merchant Ships   Full   of   Treasure :   gold,

Diamonds, Pearls.   B-ring   guns.

C U.   Love   pretty Pretty   Polly   XX XX
See you.

How do fish send messages?
They use Morse cod!

Spare Time

When not swashbuckling or buccaneering, pirates have a lot of spare time on their hands.

The best place to rest is in your hammock, but it's not the easiest thing to get into. Here are some tips.

Jump!

Climb!

Ouch!

Drop!

squidge!

If you still can't get to sleep, then lie on the edge of your hammock ... *You'll soon drop off!*

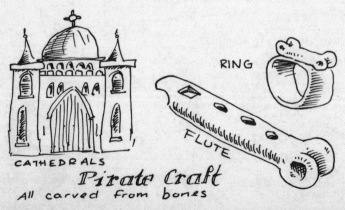

RING

CATHEDRALS

FLUTE

Pirate Craft

All carved from bones

There are all sorts of pastimes that are enjoyed by pirates. Here are a few of them.

Up the Crow's Nest

Have you seen a bunch of pirates anywhere?

No!

I wonder where the lads are tonight then.

What would you have if a pirate came at you with an axe?

An axe-i-dent!

They don't call him Mad M-axe for nothing!

Shipwreck

At any time a freak wave could smash your ship into a million pieces. It helps if you can swim, then at least you can stay afloat long enough to find some bits of wreckage that you can make a raft out of. It also helps if you sail in warm waters. Who would want to go swimming in the Arctic Ocean?

If there is sea water all around you but there's not a drop of water to drink, what do you need?

A thirst-aid kit!

> At least the world will never come to an end.

> Because it's round!

> Why?

There were once two shipwrecked survivors on a raft. The sun was so hot that they had to take it in turns to stand in each other's shadow!

There was once a band of shipwrecked pirates who managed to save a basket of homing pigeons from the wreckage. They tied strings to the pigeons' feet and let the birds tow them to the safety of the shore.

For ever after they were known as the pigeon-towed pirates!

Why do pirates always carry a bar of soap?

So, if they're shipwrecked, they can wash themselves to shore!

Cast Adrift

All alone on the ocean, clinging to a piece of wood, you've not eaten or drunk any water for three days; it's no wonder that your mind starts to imagine what may be swimming around underneath you!

Man eating shark!

What kind of fish tries to lend you money?
A loan shark!

gold fish!

Which fish eats its prey two by two?
Noah's shark!

Jelly fish!

Cross
Porpoises

Why were the dolphins angry with each other?
They were cross porpoises!

Did the pirate bump into the dolphin by accident?
No, he did it on porpoise!

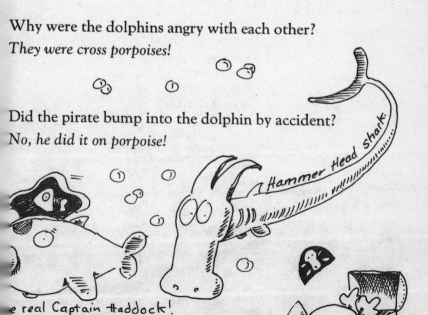

Hammer Head Shark.

...e real Captain Haddock!

Desert Islands

Why didn't the pirate get
hungry when he was left on
a desert island?

*Because of all the sand
which is there!*

Which Caribbean islands
are full of sheep?

The Baahaahaamas!

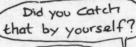

Palm
Trees

What happens if you throw
a stone into the Red Sea?

It gets wet!

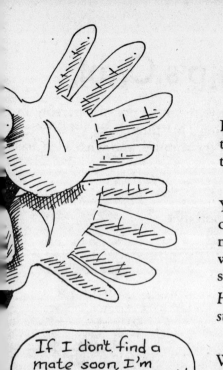

Did you know that palm trees are all fingers and thumbs?

You can go a little bit mad on a desert island. One marooned pirate would watch the reflection of the stars in the sea.

He thought they were starfish!

If I don't find a mate soon, I'm going to become extinct!

Why do dodos hide if anyone comes on to their island?

Because they're supposed to be extinct!

That's why it's called a dessert island!

The Ship's Cook

The ship's cook is not always the most popular person on board. It can't be easy feeding a bristling, hairy crew when the rats have eaten most of the supplies and what's left has gone rancid.

Most pirates live on a seafood diet.
They see food and they eat it!

What's round, green and full of bones?
A Brussels sprat!

I've never been to Belgium in my life!

Did you wash that fish before you cooked it?

What's the point? It's been in water all its life!

Here, Cookie, is it true that fish is good for the brains?
Of course. The captain eats fish every day.
Well, then, that's another theory down the drain!

Where did the ship's cook
get his sponge cakes from?
A coral reef!

The Seven Seas Quiz

Test your knowledge of the seven seas. See if you can work out the solutions to these silly clues. If you get them all correct then you should either pass your next geography exam with flying colours or promote yourself to Senior Navigator (*First Class*).

Oceans

1. Not specific.
2. Known as the Pond.
3. Probably the warmest ocean.

Seas

4. The darkest sea.
5. Not South, not East, not West.
6. The same colour as a sidetracked herring.
7. It's got three sides and things keep disappearing in it!
8. Southern pottery.
9. Could this belong to Adrian?

Geographical Features

10. You can do this with your teeth.

11. Batman wears one of these.

12. Fourth letter in the Greek alphabet.

13. A noise.

14. Wash your hands in this.

15. Sounds like a game with a little white ball.

16. Sounds like a Norwegian motor car.

Congratulations! You are now leaving the Bermuda Triangle

The answers are on page 94.

Walking the Plank

What do you do with extremely naughty pirates? What do you do with the crew of the ship you've just plundered? What do you do with the naval officers whose ship you've just sunk?

Simple. Chuck 'em over the side!

What do you call a shark
that eats a guilty pirate?
The Lord Chief Jawstice!

Monsters of the Deep

What did the giant
octopus say to his
girlfriend?

I *want* to hold *your*
hand, hand, hand,
hand, hand, hand,
hand, hand!

Which sea monster
is good at adding up?

A giant octoplus!

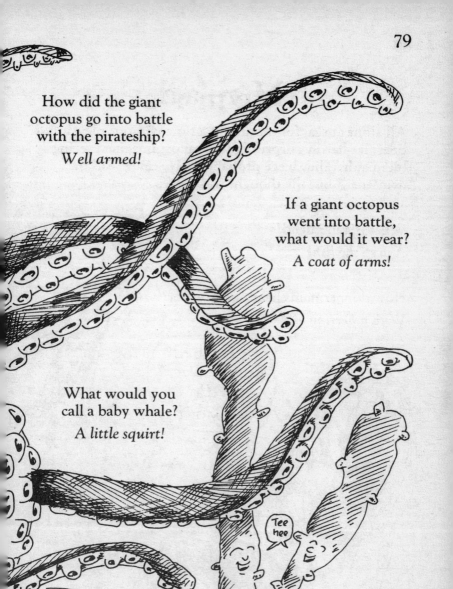

How did the giant octopus go into battle with the pirateship?

Well armed!

If a giant octopus went into battle, what would it wear?

A coat of arms!

What would you call a baby whale?

A little squirt!

Tee hee

Why was the sand wet?

Because the sea weed!

Mermaids

All alone at sea, for months at a time without their loved ones, it's hardly surprising that sailors imagined seeing mermaids. They were probably only seeing seals or manatees,* but the thought was there!

What is a mermaid?
A *deep she fish!*

How do mermaids hear under water?
With a herring aid!

* Manatees are seal-like creatures.

How big are baby mermaids?
Small scale!

What do mermaids eat for breakfast?
Toast and mermalade!

Why did the mermaid blush?
Because she saw the pirate ship's bottom!

Up the Crow's Nest

Up the Rigging

Down Among the Dead Men

At the Bottom of the Deep Blue Sea

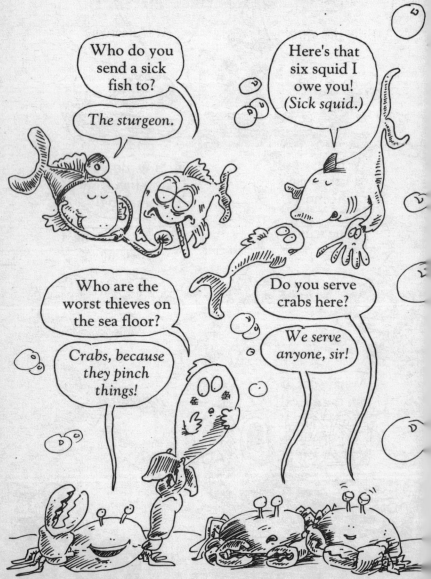

Pirate Aptitude Test

So, you still want to be a pirate? Well, here is a test to see if you have got what it takes! Each question has three answers. Ring the one that you think is correct (A, B or C), then add up your scores at the end to see if you have passed the test.

1. The pirate flag is known as:
    A. Smiling Sammy
    B. Jolly Roger
    C. Happy Harry

2. Which of the following is a ship?
    A. Stoop
    B. Sloop
    C. Scoop

3. Which do you prefer?
    A. Gold
    B. Silver
    C. Diamonds

4. What do you call the captain?
    A. Hello, sunshine!
    B. Captain, Sir!
    C. Wotcha, mate!

5.   Which end of a cannon does the shooting?
     A.   The back
     B.   The front
     C.   The middle

6.   Where would you wear an eyepatch?
     A.   On your ears
     B.   On your elbows
     C.   On your bad eye

7.   Which of the following is a cutlass?

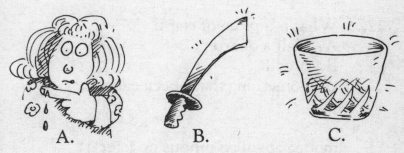

A.   B.   C.

8.   Where would you hide your treasure?
     A.   On a desert island
     B.   In an old sock in your sea chest
     C.   At the bank

9. Which of the following is a knot?
    A. A sheep's head
    B. A Turk's head
    C. A big head

10. What does maroon mean?
    A. Abandon
    B. A nice purple sort of colour
    C. Your aunty's name

11. What would you do in a hammock?
    A. Sleep in it
    B. Fall out of it
    C. Do the cat's cradle

12. What is a piece of eight?
    A. Half a quarter
    B. A coin
    C. Something that's been eaten

31-36: You should be made captain!
25-30: Apply to be first mate
19-24: Join the crew
Scores   12-18: Stay a landlubber

1. A1--B3--C2   2. A2--B3--C1   3. A2--B1--C3
4. A1--B3--C2   5. A2--B3--C1   6. A1--B2--C3
7. A2--B3--C1   8. A3--B2--C1   9. A2--B3--C1
10. A3--B2--C1   11. A3--B2--C1   12. A2--B3--C1

CERTIFICATE OF PIRACY

First Class

AWARDED TO

Captain Blackbeard

Answers

Page 23: Pirate Wordsearch Page 50: Skull and Crossword

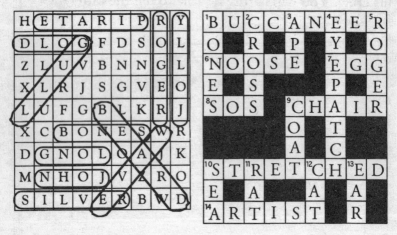

Page 74: The Seven Seas Quiz

1. Pacific 2. Atlantic 3. Indian 4. Black Sea 5. North Sea
6. Red Sea 7. The Bermuda Triangle 8. South China Sea
9. Adriatic Sea. 10. Bight 11. Cape 12. Delta 13. Sound
14. Basin 15. Gulf 16. Fiord

Do-it-yourself Pirate Sign

Just in case someone forgets to send you a pirate sign and you still fancy the pirate life, here is a do-it-yourself pirate sign that will fool any pirate captain into letting you join his crew. You will hardly be able to tell the difference from the real thing.

Trace or copy the circle below and colour it on both sides with black, waterproof Indian ink.

If anyone on board a pirate ship should challenge you, show them your pirate sign ... it is your passport to adventure!

Don't cut out of a library book! Trace it.

All the author's royalties from this book are going to The Centre for the Children's Book. So what's it all about?

British children's books are the envy of the world but, unlike some other countries, there has never been a national centre dedicated to children's books here. Instead our literary heritage is rapidly disappearing abroad as institutions all over the world snap up manuscripts and original artwork by Britain's most famous children's writers and illustrators.

To remedy this situation, The Centre for the Children's Book has been working to establish a long-needed home in Newcastle upon Tyne, where original work by the creators of children's books, from first jottings and rough sketches to finished manuscripts and artwork, will be preserved for the entire community to enjoy through exhibitions and artistic and educational programmes. It will also be a valuable resource for information and research.

This centre will celebrate the children's book and seek to place it at the heart of our literary culture by providing the nation with a unique resource, and visitors with a unique experience.

A pirate who liked a good rhyme,
Sailed up the old River Tyne,
In Newcastle he went'a,
The Children's Book Centre,
And had him a jolly good time!